Sing Your Heart Out

How to Sing
by Deborah Hudson

With Cartoons by Tony Husband

Acknowledgements
My grateful thanks to author and singer of Kapi
Christopher Hansard, Tony Husband, Wendy Lampa
and the team at Schott Music and all my teachers and
accompanists over the years.

My love and thanks to my husband Jolyon
and my son Fred.

ED 13372

British Library Cataloguing-in-Publication Data.
A catalogue record for this book is available from the
British Library.
ISBN: 978-1-84761-243-4
© 2010 Schott Music Ltd, London

Book design: adamhaystudio.com
Cover illustration: Tony Husband
Printed in Germany

Contents

Introduction

Everyone is able to sing, it's just that many of us have lost the knack. Often this happens when we're still quite small. We're informed that we are out of tune or too loud and gradually we become more and more shy so that in the end we just give up. But the impulse to sing never goes away – such self-expression is the deepest part of human nature. Up until very recently singing was a normal feature of everyday life and people didn't think twice about breaking into song on any occasion whatsoever. But now many of us are just closet singers, only having a quiet go when we think no-one else can hear. Watching talent shows on the TV and going to concerts is all very well but nothing beats the physical sensation of really singing out.

   This book will show you how you can do that. How you can sing with confidence

and power so that, if you want, you can sing anywhere you like. You don't have to be able to read music. All you need is just to give it a try!

Before You Begin

You'll need somewhere where you feel relaxed and have room enough to sit down, stand and make a noise. Have a mirror and a glass of water handy and wear some loose fitting clothes. The bathroom could work very well. If you're doing the exercises together with a friend just find a space where you both feel comfortable. Take as long as you need over each stage before proceeding onto the next one. Everyone is different but, remember, everyone can sing.

Chapter 1

Noticing How You Feel

Before you start the exercises each time, take a few minutes to notice how you are feeling and notice how your body feels to you.

Sit on a stool or a straight-backed chair with your feet firmly planted on the floor in front of you. If you prefer you could sit cross-legged on the floor. Begin to focus on each part of your body at a time. Start with the feet and move up gently through your body stopping off at each joint and ending with the tip of your nose. Do you have any aches or pains? How are you feeling emotionally? Happy? Sad? You don't need to do anything about it specially – just learn to notice,

to observe how you are. Remember
singing is expressing how all of you feels,
and if you have just stubbed your left toe
your first song might well turn into a
variation on a theme of "Ow".

Chapter 2

Squeezing and Letting Go

Staying in the sitting position put one hand on your low belly muscles (the area between your hips).

Open your mouth, gently poke your tongue forward a little so that it rests on the bottom front teeth and touches the bottom lip. *Leave it there throughout the exercise.*
Now slowly start to squeeze your belly muscles, and with your hand feel your belly being pulled in and up. At the same time notice how the air rushes

out over the tongue and out of your mouth as you squeeze.

When you feel you can't pull in any more, *leaving your mouth open and your tongue relaxed*, let those belly muscles go! Just stop squeezing.

You'll find your belly pops back out and down again and instantly air rushes back over your tongue through your mouth and into your body – quickly filling the bottom of your lungs so that you can do it all over again.

This action is the basis of what professional singers call their "support".

Do this a few times and then try saying "haaaaaaaaa" as the breath rushes out. Repeat the process so that you get used to the feeling. Then, when you are ready, try, instead of saying "haaaaaaaa", singing "haaaaa" on any note you like. You might be surprised at the strong sound. Keep going until you can't squeeze out any more breath, release the belly muscles as before, and feel the air rushing back in through the mouth.

Practise this exercise for as long as you feel comfortable and as many times a day as you like as you get used to the sensation. The sitting position should help you avoid any feelings of light-headedness and you can gradually build up the length of time of each practice as your lungs get accustomed to being used to their full extent.

Many people find the letting-go movement quite a challenge. We are encouraged by fashion to hold our bellies in and can find it hard to let go. However, you will in fact find that the squeeze and release movement actually tones the muscles wonderfully. There is often an accompanying emotional release. This is quite normal and, if you think about it, what singing is all about. The end result is that you will feel much more secure, confident and connected.

Homework

● Blow some raspberries. Go to the park and whoop! (Calling the dog might work as well.)

● The next time you see a baby cry or laugh, watch its belly muscles.

Chapter 3

Discovering Your Back

Sitting as before, make sure your back is nice and straight. Focus on your spine. Imagine walking down your spine as you might an old country railway track.

Stop occasionally and feel where you are and how the spine connects to the rest of your body. As you imagine walking up and down begin to focus on a place at the bottom of your ribs where your waist is.

When you are ready stop at this place and begin to pull in your muscles here, as if you were gently squeezing the spine. Feel how the shoulders relax, dropping down and back and how your neck straightens. It will seem as if someone has placed a hand on your back and is

supporting you. This is an excellent resting position, especially if you spend a lot of time scrunched in front of a computer. Now, with the back muscles engaged and the shoulders relaxed start squeezing the belly muscles as before. You will find that you can release the belly muscles further. Sing "haaaaaaaaa" up and down and get to know the feeling of pulling in and release with well-supported posture.

Homework

● Whenever you are standing waiting for the bus or the train think about your spine. Focus on the spine at your waist. Pull in and see how your posture suddenly improves. You will find you feel better generally – the rainy day isn't quite so depressing.

● As you sit at your desk pull in at the waist and feel the space between your shoulders and your ears. Feel the weight of the day drift from your shoulders.

Chapter 4:

Getting To Know Your Tongue

Most of us don't really think about our tongues. We know we have one, helping us to eat and form words but apart from that we don't really consider it.

In fact the tongue is very strong and reactive, especially to our fear mechanism, so it needs to be treated with respect. If you are a shy speaker and often feel "tongue tied" consider that your tongue is probably tapping into an extremely ancient and deep response – "is it safe to speak or will that animal over there hear me and have me for dinner?"

To find out more about the tongue you will need a mirror.

Once you are reasonably confident

with the breathing, sit as before but this time hold the mirror up to your face and look inside your mouth. Try singing "haaaaaa" up and down from high to low and from low to high. Does the tongue move about or curve up at the back, especially when you sing high? Do you sound or feel a little strangulated on the high notes? That tight feeling in the throat is your tongue getting in the way of the sound and air as they try to find their way out.

To relax the tongue and the jaw tilt your head right back and open your mouth as if you were going to catch raindrops. Put the tip of your tongue behind your bottom front teeth and allow it to relax down in the mouth. *Keeping your mouth and tongue in this position* bring your head back upright again and look into the mirror. Your tongue should be nice and flat and you might well see your epiglotis dangling away at the back of your mouth. Now sing "haaaaa" up and down and down and up again, keeping the tongue nice and flat as far as you can.

Notice how much louder the sound is and how much easier it is to produce.

If you are having problems relaxing the tongue try doing some "haaaaa" sounds with the tongue right out and flopped over your bottom lip like a wet towel over a sink. You may well feel a stretch as the tongue wants to pop back in, especially as you sing up and down.

Keep practising the tongue exercises a little and often and you will soon notice how much easier it is to sing high and low, and how much more easily you can hit the right note.

Homework

● Buy an ice-cream and stretch the tongue out to lick it.
● Waggle your tongue, flex it, see if you can touch your nose with it.
● Try some Tarzan noises keeping your tongue right out – see how easy it is for the sound to go up and down!

Chapter 5:

Using Your Legs and Hips

Music is made for moving around to. It affects us all physically and we naturally move in response to it.

Man's earliest songs arose from everyday activities: from the lullaby to walking, hunting and herding to planting, hauling and spinning – anything really. Up until very recently pretty much any daily repetitive task had its rhythmic song to go with it. The physical exertion of singing is something we now tend to overlook but actually it can be a great form of exercise and can still make mundane tasks much more fun to do, especially for children.

So for this next step you will need to

stand up, keeping that back nice and straight by dropping your shoulders and squeezing the waist muscles in your back, as before.

Now imagine you are rooted to the floor. Feel the weight of your body down through your legs and into your ankles and feet. Feel how the weight flows down and into the floor. Now find your relaxed jaw and tongue position by tipping your head back as before. Bring your head upright keeping the mouth open and the tongue flat and start to push down into one foot then the other, nice and rhythmically. Using the squeeze-and-release breathing technique, sing up and down on "haaaaaaaa". The extra pushing movement with the legs will give you more strength to work your belly muscles. It will also help to free up the top half of your body. You can swing your arms back and forth to help you.

Now try singing a favourite rhythmic

tune, a nursery rhyme will do. Divide it into chunks as you rhythmically push down into one leg then the other. You will find the sound is much stronger and less airy. Keep going until your muscles feel tired then take a rest. You can slowly build up the practice as you gain strength but you will gain nothing by persisting once you are tired. As you become more used to using the leg muscles in this way you will be able to monitor how much you want to move to the music. The aim is to feel how pushing down into the legs will help you engage with the sound and the song.

Homework

- You could fill the bath with grapes and tread them, singing as you work.
- Take that dog for a walk up a gentle hill, practise the technique on "haaaa" and don't worry about the strange looks!

Chapter 6:

Releasing the Words of the Song

Many of us manage fine on "haaaaa" but as soon as we start to sing words everything seizes up again.

This is often because the tongue is not working hard enough to help make the shapes which create the word sounds, but instead is simply blocking the way.

So, hang your jaw open and stand before the mirror. Now, without moving the jaw or lips see if you can make certain consonants just by moving the tongue against the roof of your mouth. Try "ttt", "ddd", "lll", "kkk", "ggg". Make sure you drop the tongue down between each letter. You will find that the tongue actually needs to work quite hard! When you have tried this for a bit add the vowel sound "ah" to make "tah tah tah", "dah dah dah", "lah lah lah", "kah kah kah", "gah gah gah". Practise this whenever you have a moment.

Think of a very simple song and sing the tune on "gah", making sure you drop the back of the tongue down after each "g". Feel the strength of the sound!

Now introduce the words by speaking them keeping the jaw relaxed and making the tongue work as much as possible. If you choose something like *Twinkle Twinkle Little Star* you will find that you can pronounce most of it with your mouth open and without actually moving the jaw or lips at all.

Try singing the words in the same way. Feel and hear how much the song can freely emerge from your mouth. Finally sing the song complete, using the lips

when you need to but making the tongue do the hard work. Feel how much easier it is!

As a rule, the more energy you can put into pronouncing the consonants the easier you will find singing to be. You can squeeze in the belly muscles a little extra on main consonants just to make sure you are truly connected.

Homework

● Sing a song as if you were singing it to someone on the other side of the main road and who couldn't understand your language very well. Emphasise the consonants and make the tongue work hard.

● With some friends try and have a conversation without moving the jaw and the lips. How much can you be understood by just using the tongue?

Chapter 7:

Listening

Sounds can be a bit like smells – we find some pleasant, some distressing and both can be pretty invasive.

Which sounds do you welcome and which do you try and fend off? We all of us try to resist certain sounds and certain tones of voice. Remember the maxim "don't ask a question unless you are prepared to listen to the answer"? How many of us have at some time made up our minds about a situation in advance, so have closed our ears to explanations. Early in life the anger in the tones of an exasperated teacher can make us freeze up inside and block out what the teacher is trying to say. General anxiousness can impede our hearing so we become muddled and don't know how to reply.

This in turn produces more nervousness.

Equally, perhaps the sound of your own voice has frightened or distracted you. All of these emotions will cause our tongues to stiffen but they can often also prevent us being able properly to listen.

So for this exercise find somewhere comfortable and safe to sit or lie down in and simply listen to all the sounds around you. Explore them and allow them to enter your body. See if you can focus on one particular sound then on another. Can you hear the sound of a bird, a person laughing, a dog barking? Get used to listening without the stress of needing to respond in a particular way. Our ears are formed very early on in our development and we learn to interpret tones of voice way before we manage to understand language. See if you can distinguish between the tone of what someone is communicating and the words they use. Notice how you feel, but let the sounds come and go.

Once you are comfortable with this process try copying some of the sounds you hear. It could be the sound of a tap dripping, it could be next door's cat – the point is to hear and then gradually to mimic. This is what we all did when we began to learn language. Discover that process again – feel what your tongue is doing too to imitate these sounds. Make friends with them.

When you feel ready, resume the standing-to-sing position and ask a friend to sing a note for you or you can find a simple musical sound to copy. *Using the techniques you have learned*, sing out what you hear. By listening and singing back in this focussed, stress-free and well-supported way you will be able to match your sound to what you hear. Singing along with the radio or with your favourite CD will suddenly be much, much simpler.

Chapter 8:

Connecting and Communicating

As we said right at the beginning, singing is about communicating how you feel about something.

You now know how to make a good strong sound that will carry, but what message do your eyes convey? Where are you looking? Making even fleeting eye contact with another person as you sing can be quite a challenge, so start off by singing to yourself.

Sing your song to your reflection in the mirror and as you do so allow the intent of what you are singing to come through your eyes. Allow them to communicate the emotion you feel. Practise this until you feel confident looking at

yourself in the eyes and then check the rest of your posture. If you are squeezing the back muscles your posture will be strong and good to look at. Lift the chest a little more so you feel it is nice and open. Don't poke your head forward so remember, "chest before chin"! Imagine you're wearing a beautiful diamond necklace, have a luxurious cleavage or are exposing the most stunningly muscular chest. Now sing out! Sing your song to yourself and enjoy the sensation.

Chapter 9

Where To Go From Here

Now that you have a strong sound and can sing with confidence the world is of course your oyster.

Keep practising the exercises regularly to strengthen the muscles and develop your sound. You can carry on singing along to music in the shower or perhaps you might like to join a group or choir. Singing with a large group, for example at a football match, is an excellent way to practise singing out. Remember always to project your songs using those low belly muscles – don't be tempted to shout! If you are thinking of joining a choir ask the choir leader if you can warm up by singing some simple rounds.

These are very useful to help you keep focussed on your own voice and technique while learning how to be aware of others. There are lots of possibilities. Further singing training is of course an option if you discover you really want to explore your voice a little more. The Association of Teachers of Singing has a website you can consult to find a teacher. Make sure whoever you choose is someone you like and feel comfortable with – the hard work should always be a pleasure. But, above all else, have fun!

Note

All the exercises in this book have been well tried and tested in practice. Some refer back to very old singing traditions, some to the Italian *bel canto* tradition and some to more recent singing techniques.

I find *Healing Songs* and *Work Songs* both by Ted Gioia paticularly interesting books. *Kum Nye: Waking Up for Beginners* by S. Wright describes an excellent physical exercise system which I do, and which is very useful for singers. For further information and further reading please consult my website www.singdeborahhudson.com.

About the Author

Deborah teaches singing to all people at all levels, both able-bodied and disabled. She also teaches in-house corporate groups and trains therapists, school volunteers and teachers. Deborah has studied many singing methods, most particularly *bel canto* techniques, and has performed all styles of music as an opera singer, recitalist, session singer, soloist and chorister.

As a freelance writer her work has appeared in a number of publications including the *Times Literary Supplement*, *The Economist Magazine*, *The Guardian*, *Homes and Gardens*, *Apollo* and *Orientations* Magazines. She has edited a book of poetry, translated songs and operetta for recital programmes and has written several musical farces.

About the Illustrator

Tony Husband's cartoons have appeared in many newspapers, magazines, books and websites, and in several TV and theatrical productions. They include *Private Eye*, *The Times*, *Punch*, *Playboy*, *The Sunday Express*, *The Spectator* and *The Sun*. He has won more than 15 major awards, including the Pont Award for depicting the British way of life.

In the 1980s, he co-devised and edited *Oink!*, a popular children's comic and its TV spin-off, *Round The Bend*, for Hat Trick Productions. For the theatre, he co-wrote a play and accompanying book, *Save The Human*, with David Wood. He and the poet Ian McMillan tour the UK regularly with their show *A Cartoon History Of Here*, an evening of live, improvised poetry and cartoons.

Continue to *Sing Your Heart Out* with these titles from Schott Music

Tona de Brett
Discover Your Voice

ED 12498
ISBN 978-0-946535-30-9

Renowned singing teacher, Tona de Brett, presents her teaching material, as used with stars of rock, jazz and musicals. Various aspects of voice-production are dealt with through a wealth of exercises and examples. The *Working in the Studio* section by Tom West helps singers prepare for the recording studio.

Klaus Heizmann
Vocal Warm-ups

ED 9564
ISBN 978-3-7957-5259-0

200 exercises for choral and solo singers.
Designed to do more than just warm up the voice, these exercises help to relax the body, train the ear and develop an awareness of dynamics and rhythm.

The **Best Of** Series

Best of Folk Songs
ED 12880 | ISBN 978-1-84761-032-4 *
ED 12881 | ISBN 978-1-902455-73-0 †

Best of Canons & Rounds
ED 13170 | ISBN 978-1-84761-116-1 **

Best of Children's Songs
ED 12948 | ISBN 978-1-902455-83-9 *
ED 12949 | ISBN 978-1-902455-84-6 †

Best of Gilbert & Sullivan
ED 13063 | ISBN 978-1-84761-047-8 ††

Best of Christmas Carols
ED 12766 | ISBN 978-1-902455-11-2 *
ED 12808 | ISBN 978-1-902455-12-9 †

Best of Spirituals & Gospels
ED 9451 | ISBN 978-3-7957-5754-0 *
ED 9643 | ISBN 978-3-7957-5645-1 †

* Piano, Voice & Guitar	** Voice only
† Voice & Guitar	†† Voice & Piano

Collections and arrangements of favourite songs from
different genres available in editions with easy-to-play
piano accompaniments and guitar chords

Available from your local music shop or from www.schott-music.co.uk

John Kember

Sight-Singing

Volume 1
ED 12737 | ISBN 978-1-84761-253-3

Volume 2
ED 12790 | ISBN 978-1-902455-22-8

Master the art of singing at sight with these two volumes of exercices by John Kember.

A progressive approach takes you from the basics through to more advanced sight reading.

Designed to instil confidence in singers and to present a method of approaching all aspects of singing at sight.

Available from your local music shop or from www.schott-music.co.uk